S0-BBY-616

BOOKS BY W. S. MERWIN

POEMS

The Rain in the Trees   *1988*
Selected Poems   *1988*
Opening the Hand   *1983*
Finding the Islands   *1982*
The Compass Flower   *1977*
The First Four Books of Poems   *1975*
(INCLUDING THE COMPLETE TEXTS OF
*A Mask for Janus, The Dancing Bears,
Green with Beasts* AND *The Drunk in the Furnace*)
Writings to an Unfinished Accompaniment   *1973*
The Carrier of Ladders   *1970*
The Lice   *1967*
The Moving Target   *1963*
The Drunk in the Furnace   *1960*
Green With Beasts   *1956*
The Dancing Bears   *1954*
A Mask for Janus   *1952*

PROSE

Unframed Originals   *1982*
Houses and Travellers   *1977*
The Miner's Pale Children   *1970*

TRANSLATIONS

Four French Plays   *1985*
From the Spanish Morning   *1985*
Selected Translations 1968–1978   *1979*
Osip Mandelstam, Selected Poems
(WITH CLARENCE BROWN)   *1974*
Asian Figures   *1973*
Transparence of the World (Poems by Jean Follain)   *1969*
Voices (Poems by Antonio Porchia)   *1969;*
revised and enlarged edition   *1988*
*Products of the Perfected Civilization
(Selected Writings of Chamfort)*   *1969*
*Twenty Love Poems and a Song of Despair
(Poems by Pablo Neruda)*   *1969*
Selected Translations 1948–1968   *1968*
The Song of Roland   *1963*
The Satires of Persius   *1960*
The Poem of the Cid   *1959*

VOICES

VOICES

APHORISMS BY

ANTONIO PORCHIA

A REVISED AND ENLARGED
SELECTION TRANSLATED BY

W. S. MERWIN

ALFRED A KNOPF   NEW YORK
1988

THIS IS A BORZOI BOOK
PUBLISHED BY ALFRED A. KNOPF, INC.

Copyright © 1969 by W. S. Merwin
Revised and enlarged edition copyright © 1988
by W. S. Merwin

All rights reserved under International and Pan-American
Copyright Conventions. Published in the United States by
Alfred A. Knopf, Inc., New York, and simultaneously in
Canada by Random House of Canada Limited, Toronto. Dis-
tributed by Random House, Inc., New York.

Library of Congress Cataloging-in-Publication Data

Porchia, Antonio.
Voices : aphorisms.

Translation of: Voces.
I. Merwin, W. S. (William Stanley), [date]. II. Title.
PQ7797.P665V6213   1988   868   87–46238
ISBN 0–394–75884–6 (pbk.)

Manufactured in the United States of America
First Edition

A NOTE ON ANTONIO PORCHIA

"I know what I have given you.
I do not know what you have received."

THE FIRST collection of Porchia's *Voices* appeared in Buenos Aires, in a private edition, in 1943, and attracted little attention. A copy was sent by the author to the French critic Roger Caillois, who was moved to translate a selection of the aphorisms and publish them, with an introduction, in 1949. The somewhat patronizing tone in which Caillois presented his discovery did not conceal a sense of having been given a rare and original work, and the aphorisms themselves, in

his versions, found at the time a number of ad-
mirers in the French literary world.

Caillois, wanting to find out what sort of man
had written and sent this surprising volume, had
looked into the matter and "found myself in the
presence of a man somewhere in his fifties, re-
spectably—though neither studiously nor elegant-
ly—dressed; a potter or carpenter by trade, I forget which, and self-employed, what is more; at
once simple and shy, and altogether such that I
assured myself, simply as a formality, first by
means of certain subterfuges, and then quite open-
ly, that he had never in his life heard of Lao-Tzu
or Kafka." (By whom Caillois had suspected his
unknown author to be influenced.)

Judging by Caillois' observations, the remarkable
content of the *Voices* is in a peculiarly pure sense
the product of Porchia's own non-literary experience. Of this, or of its circumstances, little is pub-
licly known beyond a few facts so bare that they
would fit on any tombstone. Antonio Porchia was
born in Italy in 1886, lived in Argentina from
1911, and died in 1968. *Voices* represents the
whole of his writing—some six hundred entries in
all. There have been several editions since the first
one. The most recent (and in Porchia's judgment
the most complete, though it does not include some
from the first collection) was published in 1966,

and it is from this edition that the present selection has been made. Some of the entries, Porchia has stated, evolved over the course of years; some he has deleted in favor of later ones which, in his opinion, convey the same sense better. But the aphorisms themselves are not, in his view, compositions of his own so much as emanations which he has heard and set down.

It is easy to see why Caillois might have imagined that Porchia owed something to certain Eastern texts, and perhaps to some moderns such as Kafka. A few of the aphorisms have close affinities with sentences from Taoist and Buddhist scriptures; others suggest, among the moderns, not only Kafka but Lichtenberg, or—to someone whose language is English—Blake. Caillois' determining, to his own satisfaction, that Porchia was unfamiliar with such possible mentors is interesting, surprising, and in the end remains for the most part a matter of curiosity rather than a contribution to an assessment of the values and originality of Porchia's *Voices*. For the authority which the entries invoke, both in their matter and in their tone, is not that of tradition or antecedents, but that of particular, individual experience. Whatever system may be glimpsed binding the whole together is not fashioned from any logic except that of one man's cast of existence. It is this which makes the work as a whole, and some of the separate sentences, elusive, but it is this which gives them this unmistakable pure immediacy—their quality of voice.

At the same time, the entries and the work as a whole assume and evoke the existence of an absolute, of the knowledge of it which is truth, and of the immense desirability of such knowledge. With no doctrinal allegiances, nor any attempt at dogmatic system, Porchia's utterances are obviously, in this sense, a spiritual, quite as much as a literary, testament. And the center to which they bear witness, as well as the matrix of their form, is the private ordeal and awe of individual existence, the reality that is glimpsed through time and circumstance, as a consequence of feeling and suffering. It is this ground of personal revelation and its logic, in the sentences, that marks their kinship, not with theology but with poetry.

And yet the reality of the self, except as suffering, is not an unquestionable certainty. "My final belief is suffering. And I begin to believe that I do not suffer." In any event, the "self" that we take for granted depends upon other things. "We see by means of something which illumines us, which we do not see." But the fidelity of Porchia's vision and its embodiment in language are too intimate to be tempted to homiletics. Instead the distillate of suffering in some of the entries is pure and profound irony—an irony not of defense but of acceptance. "Every toy has the right to break."

"When I throw away what I don't want, it will fall within reach." It is finally the acceptance, with its irony, that underlies the suffering and the vision and relates them to each other in a way that suggests that the relation may be the privilege of man's existence. "Man goes nowhere. Everything comes to man, like tomorrow."

W. S. MERWIN (1969)

NOTES TO THE REVISED
AND ENLARGED EDITION

W H E N I translated most of the aphorisms in this collection and wrote the foregoing introductory note in the late 1960's, I knew the definitive text of Porchia's *Voices*, which he had sent me, but of Porchia himself I knew only the few, rather indefinite details in the introduction to Roger Caillois' French translation. It was clear that for Caillois as well Porchia the man was something of a mystery. Porchia was an old man by then, and evidently in rather precarious health. His few letters were delicate and courteous, written in ink in an angular, elegant, plain, but somewhat frail hand. They were not stiff or forbidding, but they were slightly formal and they were brief. They did not suggest the likelihood of a voluminous correspondence brimming with biography. Porchia's publishing arrangements, by then, and evidently some of the practical affairs of his life, were being looked after, at least in part, by a writer named D. J. Vogelmann, in Buenos Aires, evidently a kind and generous person, but the business-like nature of the correspondence with him did not promise much revelation of Porchia's history, and whatever I attempted by way of direct questioning elicited nothing. In 1967 I managed to obtain funding for the fare to Buenos Aires, and while I was still putting together a sum to live on while I was there I wrote to Sr. Vogelmann about coming. Before I could leave, he wrote back that Porchia was very sick, and then that he was dead.

A few years later I was attracted to the poetry of another writer from Argentina, Roberto Juarroz, and began translating him and corresponding with him. Juarroz had dedicated a poem to Porchia, and I asked what he had known about the older man. It turned out that during Porchia's later years Juarroz, and his wife, the writer Laura Cerrato, had been among Porchia's intimate and devoted friends, and that both had written about Porchia's work. Juarroz, besides, had published some discreet reminiscences of his friend, and I am indebted to his generosity for these few glimpses of a rare nature, a man whose integrity and humility did not spare him from becoming a figure of controversy in the little circles of literary fashion in the Buenos Aires of the '50's and '60's—for which, after all, he had never written.

Porchia was born, as I knew, in Italy. Juarroz says ("Antonio Porchia O La Profundidad Recuperada," *Plural*, Mexico; Vol. IV, no. 11, Aug. 1975) that his birthplace was Calabria, and that Porchia's father had been a priest who had left his calling and had been forced, as a result, to endure years of uncertainty and insecurity. Porchia's underlying memory of his childhood was its shifting, unsettled character. The family never stayed in one place for long. In his later years he spoke little of either of his parents, though he refers to them both in his aphorisms.

When Porchia left Italy for Argentina, in his twenties, he worked first as a clerk in the port of Buenos Aires, and then for years in a printing house. Juarroz says that he never heard Porchia express the slightest discontent with his lot. But then, "I never saw him impatient or anxious about financial difficulties." Nor, Juarroz adds, about the obtuseness and jealousy that tried to prevent Porchia's work from being recognized. "He was in no hurry for anything."

Juarroz remembers with particular awe what he calls Porchia's "unusual and deepening attention." "When we were with him we heard each word deepen under his boundless attention. His way of listening seemed to create a depth in his companions. And when he spoke we had the feeling that he did so 'from the other side', which then became infinitely close, much closer than this side."

"One day he told me that when he was a very small child, and hungry, he had started playing with a ball, and had jumped and fallen down in a faint. From that he concluded that hunger was no obstacle to happiness."

One afternoon, Juarroz recalls, he and Porchia were walking along the Calle de La Boca, one of Porchia's favorite parts of the city, and one of the poorest—small houses painted in all kinds of colors, immigrants from everywhere, sounds of the port, voices and music out of the bars full of sailors and longshoremen. Porchia had just been to see a woman with whom he had been in love, and who was then old and alone and sick. "To keep someone company," he had said to Juarroz, "is not just to be with them but to be within them." At one time he had been in love with a woman of ill repute, and had wanted to marry her, but their relation had led to her being threatened, and they had given up seeing each other.

But "we always felt," Juarroz writes, "that we were in the presence of someone chosen for solitude." Yet Porchia did not "compensate for that with literature or the facile company of others, but with the depth of his own life. His solitude allowed him to arrive at being more completely with others, as though from underneath. With him we learned how solitude can be the opposite of isolation."

"The houses in which we went to call on him grew smaller and smaller, after he had to sell the one his brother left him and buy a cheaper one, farther from the center of town, so that he could subsist for a while on the difference. But he always kept every one of the paintings that had been given to him by painter friends—among them some of the most celebrated Argentine painters of this century. . . He never gave up one of them, not even at times of extreme poverty, when some of his friends and associates tried to persuade him to sell one or two of them. He said that he lived alone and needed almost nothing. It is clear that he could not sell what had been a gift."

"I do not remember another being who was so simple and so graceful. He almost never wore a shirt. In the summer he put on a pyjama jacket and in the winter he tucked a scarf under a heavier coat, holding it in place with a hair pin. When we were with him he set out on his table a bottle of wine and a bit of cheese, salami, and bread, which he had been to the market to buy, out of his slender purse."

"When certain members of the arts institute in which he had placed almost the entire edition of his first book grumbled about the space it took up, he quietly turned it over to the public libraries."

Juarroz was not present when Porchia died. Porchia had fallen and struck his head, on a week-end outing in the country, where he had been taken by some new friends. Apparently he did not recover from the concussion. Shortly before his death he had been recorded reading from his *Voices*, and for some time after he died his voice was used by a Buenos Aires radio station, each night as it signed off. In Porchia's slow, deep utterance, Juarroz remembers, there was still a trace of a foreign accent.

W. S. MERWIN (1988)

VOICES

S I T U A T E D in some nebulous distance I do
what I do so that the universal balance of
which I am a part may remain a balance.

He who has seen everything empty itself is
close to knowing what everything is filled
with.

Before I travelled my road I was my road.

I found the whole of my first world in my meager bread.

My father, when he went, made my childhood a gift of a half a century.

The little things are what is eternal, and the rest, all the rest, is brevity, extreme brevity.

Without this ridiculous vanity that takes the form of self-display, and is part of everything and everyone, we would see nothing, and nothing would exist.

Truth has very few friends and those few are suicides.

Treat me as you should treat me, not as I should be treated.

Man goes nowhere. Everything comes to men, like tomorrow.

He who holds me by a thread is not strong; the thread is strong.

A little candor never leaves me. It is what protects me.

A door opens to me. I go in and am faced with a hundred closed doors.

My poverty is not complete: it lacks me.

If you do not raise your eyes you will think that you are the highest point.

In no one did I find who I should be like. And I stayed like that: like no one.

Not believing has a sickness which is believing a little.

I know that you have nothing. That is why I ask you for everything. So that you will have everything.

I come from dying, not from having been born. From having been born I am going.

Out of a hundred years a few minutes were made that stayed with me, not a hundred years.

One lives in the hope of becoming a memory.

I have scarcely touched clay and I am made of it.

I believe that the soul consists of its sufferings.
For the soul that cures its own sufferings dies.

Man talks about everything, and he talks about
everything as though the understanding of
everything were all inside him.

Nothing that is complete breathes.

A great deal that I no longer continue, within
myself, continues there on its own.

Yes, they are mistaken, because they do not
know. And if they knew . . . Nothing. They
would not even be mistaken.

Everything is like the rivers: the work of the
slopes.

When I am asleep I dream what I dream when I am awake. It's a continuous dream.

The summits guide, but among summits.

They have stopped deceiving you, not loving you. And it seems to you that they have stopped loving you.

Sometimes it is as though I were in a hell, and I do not grieve. I do not find anything to grieve over.

A ray of light erased your name. Now I do not know who you are.

It is when I assent to nothing that I assent to all.

Man, when he is merely what he seems to be, is almost nothing.

You will find the distance that separates you
from them, by joining them.

A hundred men together are the hundredth
part of a man.

When the superficial wearies me, it wearies
me so much that I need an abyss in order to
rest.

Not everyone does evil, but everyone stands
accused.

What we pay for with our lives never costs
too much.

I will help you to approach if you approach,
and to keep away if you keep away.

He who does not fill his world with phantoms remains alone.

Sometimes I find that misery is so vast that I am afraid of needing it.

You think you are killing me. I think you are committing suicide.

The grieving for everyone and about everything has grown and become a grieving for myself, to myself. And it is still growing.

The far away, the very far, the farthest, I have found only in my own blood.

The mystery brings peace to my eyes, not blindness.

When your suffering is a little greater than
my suffering I feel that I am a little cruel.

He who tells the truth says almost nothing.

A thing, until it is everything, is noise, and
once it is everything it is silence.

Mud, when it leaves the mud, stops being mud.

For a thousand years I have been asking
myself, "What will I do now?" And still I
need not answer.

Nothing is not only nothing. It is also our
prison.

When I come upon some idea that is not of
this world, I feel as though this world had
grown wider.

My heaviness comes from the heights.

The earth has what you raise from the earth.
It has nothing more.

Only the wound speaks its own word.

A new pain enters and the old pains of the
household receive it with their silence, not
with their death.

Yes, I will try to be. Because I believe that
not being is arrogant.

That in man which cannot be domesticated is
not his evil but his goodness.

Day cannot mock him who does not mock
the night.

No, I will not go in. Because if I go in there is no one.

Nothing—it is said of this, of that, of almost everything. Only it is never said of nothing.

I love for the sake of what I loved, and what I loved I would not go back to loving.

When I believe that the stone is stone and the cloud cloud, I am in a state of unconsciousness.

The flower that you hold in your hands was born today and already it is as old as you are.

Sometimes I think that everything I see does not exist. Because everything I see is what I saw. And everything that I saw does not exist.

Chimeras come singly and leave accompanied.

There are sufferings that have lost their
memory and do not remember why they are
suffering.

Man, when he does not grieve, hardly exists.

They will say that you are on the wrong road,
if it is your own.

A wing is neither heaven nor earth.

We have a world for each one, but we do not
have a world for all.

Injury, when it is slight, bothers me; when
it is strong it calms me.

Nothing ends without breaking, because
everything is endless.

I have come one step away from everything.
And here I stay, far from everything, one step
away.

All the suns labor to kindle your flame and a
microbe puts it out.

More grievous than tears is the sight of them.

Man is air in the air and in order to become a
point in the air he has to fall.

Would there be this eternal seeking if the
found existed?

Suffering does not follow us. It goes before us.

We tear life out of life to use it for looking at
itself.

For as long as and insofar as it cannot be, it is almost always a reproach to everything that can.

This world understands nothing but words, and you have come into it with almost none.

He who remains with himself a great deal becomes debased.

We become aware of the void as we fill it.

God has given a great deal to man, but man would like something from man.

When everything is finished, the mornings are sad.

Following straight lines shortens distances, and also life.

In full light we are not even a shadow.

Everyone thinks that his things are not like all the things in the world. And that is why everyone keeps them.

When there is no treasure to show, night is a treasure.

The tree is alone, the cloud is alone. Everything is alone when I am alone.

A hundred years die in a moment, just as a moment dies in a moment.

Suffering is above, not below. And everyone thinks that suffering is below. And everyone wants to rise.

My body separates me from every being and from every thing. Nothing but my body.

Sometimes at night I light a lamp so as not to see.

He who is imprisoned in evil does not escape from it for fear of encountering—evil.

If you are not going to change your route, why change your guide?

The less a creature thinks he is, the more he bears. And if he thinks he is nothing, he bears all.

I saw a dead man. And I was little, little, little . . . My God, what a great thing a dead man is!

Yes, one must suffer, even in vain, so as not to have lived in vain.

No one understands that you have given everything. You must give more.

The killer of souls does not kill a hundred souls. He kills one soul a hundred times.

He who does not know how to believe, should not know.

Only a few arrive at nothing, because the way is long.

I am in myself so little that what they do with me scarcely interests me.

Where we have put something we always believe that there is something, though there may be nothing there.

If only I could leave everything as it is, without moving a single star or a single cloud. Oh, if only I could!

Certainties are arrived at only on foot.

Man, when he realizes that he is an object of comedy, does not laugh.

In my silence only my voice is missing.

Human suffering, while it is asleep, is shapeless. If it is wakened it takes the form of the waker.

My truths do not last long in me. Not as long as those that are not mine.

A child shows his toy, a man hides his.

Some things become so completely our own that we forget them.

I love you as you are, but do not tell me how that is.

If I did not believe that the sun looked at me a little bit, I would not look at it.

The confession of one humbles all.

Near me nothing but distances.

When I die, I will not see myself die, for the first time.

Your suffering is so great that it must not hurt you.

My faults will not pass into other hands through any fault of mine. I do not want another fault on my hands.

Yes, I will go. I would rather grieve over your absence than over you.

When you made me into another, I left you with me.

It is a long time now since I asked heaven for anything, and still my arms have not come down.

I know what I have given you. I do not know
what you have received.

The shadows: some hide, others reveal.

The heart is an infinity of massive chains,
chaining little handfuls of air.

Set out from any point. They are all alike.
They all lead to a point of departure.

You are fastened to them and cannot understand how, because they are not fastened to
you.

When I see myself I ask, "What do others
think they see?"

I do not want anything over again. Not even
a mother.

The loss of a thing affects us until we have lost it altogether.

Yes, this is what good is: to forgive evil. There is no other good.

You are sad because they abandon you and you have not fallen.

Whatever I take, I take too much or too little; I do not take the exact amount. The exact amount is no use to me.

The cold is a good counsellor, but it is cold.

I do not believe in exceptions. Because I believe that nothing comes from a single thing. Not even solitude.

The void terrifies you, and you open your
eyes wider!

When one does not love the impossible, one
does not love anything.

All that I know does not even help me to
know it.

Everything is a little bit of darkness, even the
light.

Yes, I am preoccupied with myself. But I have
forgotten what that means.

I am not of your mind. But if you are not of
your mind either, then I am of your mind.

Some things, in order to show me their lack
of existence, became mine.

Not using faults does not mean that one does not have them.

You have nothing and you want to give me a world. I owe you a world.

The blind man carries a star on his shoulders.

I know that I went from the brief before to the eternal afterward of everything, but I do not know how.

Man lives measuring and he is measured by nothing. Not even by himself.

My dignity asks him who does me no harm to do me no harm. Of him who harms me it asks nothing.

All that I have lost I find at every step and re-member that I have lost it.

My pieces of time play with eternity.

My final belief is suffering. And I begin to believe that I do not suffer.

And if man were good, his goodness would be the same as nothing. For it would cost him nothing.

I am chained to the earth to pay for the freedom of my eyes.

To wound the heart is to create it.

The fear of separation is all that unites.

When I look for my existence I do not look
for it in myself.

If those who owe us nothing gave us nothing,
how poor we would be.

If I forgot what I have not been, I would
forget myself.

When you seem to be listening to my words,
they seem to be your words, with me listening.

In its last moment the whole of my life will
last only a moment.

When I have nothing left, I will ask for no
more.

The soul of all is only the soul of each one.

It is easier for me to see everything as one
thing than to see one thing as one thing.

Every time I wake I understand how easy it is
to be nothing.

I would go to heaven, but I would take my
hell; I would not go alone.

He who goes up step by step always finds
himself level with a step.

Everything that changes, where it changes,
leaves behind it an abyss.

You are a puppet, but in the hands of the
infinite, which may be your own.

Everything is becoming the same. And that
is how everything ends: becoming the same.

Among the superficial, if you are not one of them, one of them has to lead you by the hand.

Man is weak and when he makes strength his profession he is weaker.

Real things exist while we attribute to them virtues or defects of unreal things.

The tragedy of man is greater when he gives it up.

Where everyone grieves no one hears the crying.

The sun illumines the night, it does not turn it into light.

When I throw away what I don't want, it will fall within reach.

Every toy has the right to break.

Everything that I bear within me bound, is to be found somewhere else free.

They are like me, I tell myself. And in that way I defend myself against them. And in that way I defend myself against myself.

The things of mine that are utterly lost are the ones that, when I lost them, were not found by someone else.

I have been my own disciple and my own master. And I have been a good disciple but a bad master.

No-one can help going beyond. And beyond there is an abyss.

My dead go on suffering in me the pain of living.

I stop wanting what I am looking for, looking for it.

I also had a summer and burned myself in its name.

A full heart has room for everything and an empty heart has room for nothing. Who understands?

They owe you life and a box of matches, and they want to pay you a box of matches, because they don't want to owe you a box of matches.

When I believe in nothing I do not want to meet you when you believe in nothing.

Sometimes I believe that evil is everything, and that good is only a beautiful desire for evil.

Since I prepare only for what ought to happen to me, I am never ready for what does happen. Never.

The taste of "mine" is not bitter, but it nourishes no one.

And if you still find something, you have not lost everything. You still have to lose something.

The children whom nobody leads by the hand are the children who know they are children.

A large heart can be filled with very little.

If you could escape from your sufferings, and did so, where would you go outside them?

The love that is not all pain is not all love.

One learns not to need by needing.

If I were someone who led himself I would not take the path that leads to death.

I hold up what I know with what I do not know.

And if the clouds think they fly with their wings, they fly with their wings, but they cannot control them.

The condemnation of an error is another error.

Words that they said to me at other times, I hear now.

As long as we think we are worth something, we wrong ourselves.

My name, far more than it names me, reminds me of my name.

When I break any of the chains that bind me I feel that I make myself smaller.

And why should I regret what I have done when I cannot help doing what I do, which is what I have done?

I keep my hands empty for the sake of what
I have had in them.

Now humanity does not know where to go,
because no one is waiting for it: not even
God.

I have abandoned the beggarly necessity of
living. I live without it.

He who does not find a fountain through
which to pour his tears, does not weep.

My "I" has gone farther and farther away
from me. Today it is my farthest "you."

You are always telling a dream. When do you
dream it?

Now you do not know what to do, not even
when you go back to being a child. And it is
sad to see a child who does not know what to
do.

He who has made a thousand things and he
who has made none, both feel the same desire:
to make something.

If I were to give you life, what could I give
you?

When I approach a soul I do not take with
me a desire to become acquainted with it; when
I go away from one, I do.

When I do not walk in the clouds I walk as
though I were lost.

The virtues of a thing do not come from it:
they go to it.

The harm that I have not done, what harm
it has done!

Everywhere my side is the left. I was born on
that side.

When they call me "my," I am no one.

Even the smallest of creatures carries a sun in
its eyes.

If you are good to this one and that one, this
one and that one will say that you are good. If
you are good to everyone, no one will say
that you are good.

He who makes a paradise of his bread makes
a hell of his hunger.

There was no mistake this time. And this time
I was afraid of everything.

The irreparable is the act of no one: it happens
by itself.

I would ask something more of this world,
if it had something more.

It is less degrading to fear than to be feared.

Those who gave away their wings are sad not
to see them fly.

You do not see the river of tears because it
lacks one tear of your own.

My neighbor's poverty makes me feel poor;
my own does not.

We see by means of something which
illumines us, which we do not see.

Do not speak harshly of your misfortunes to
anyone, because everyone is partly to blame.

Who has seen with the eyes open can see
again, but with the eyes closed.

If flowers appear out of season, do not let
them grow.

You can owe nothing, if you give back its
light to the sun.

My great day came and went, I do not know
how. Because it did not pass through dawn
when it came, nor through dusk when it
went.

That which was before me and that which
comes after me have almost come together,
they have almost become one thing, they have
almost been left without me.

I began my comedy as its only actor, and I
come to the end of it as its only spectator.

In the eternal dream, eternity is the same as
an instant. Maybe I will come back in an
instant.

In that world I knew that good was killing
me, but I thought it was evil.

What I say to myself—who says it? Who does
he say it to?

And if you find everything as soon as you
look for it, you find it in vain, you look for it
in vain.

I am in yesterday, today. And tomorrow? In tomorrow I was.

The dream which is not fed with dream disappears.

Everything is nothing, but afterwards. After having suffered everything.

Night is a world lit by itself.

Almost always it is the fear of being ourselves that brings us to the mirror.

Because they know the name of what I am looking for, they think they know what I am looking for!

When you and the truth speak to me I do not listen to the truth. I listen to you.

I can wait for you no longer. Because you
have arrived.

Beyond my body my veins are invisible.

The chains that bind us most closely are the
ones we have broken.

To be someone is to be someone alone.
To be someone is solitude.

What words say does not last. The words last.
Because words are always the same, and
what they say is never the same.

You wound and you will wound again.
Because you wound and then you go away.
You do not stay with the wound.

To the best of refuges I prefer their doorways.

The real "it is well" is something I say from the ground, having fallen.

The important and the unimportant are the same only at the start.

All truth acts out from the new-born. From that which was not.

Flowers are without hope. Because hope is tomorrow and flowers have no tomorrow.

He is small who hides in order to show himself.

It was always easier for me to love than to praise.

A NOTE ABOUT THE TRANSLATOR

W. S. Merwin was born in New York City in 1927 and grew up in Union City, New Jersey, and in Scranton, Pennsylvania. From 1949 to 1951 he worked as a tutor in France, Portugal, and Majorca. After that, for several years he made the greater part of his living by translating from French, Spanish, Latin and Portuguese. Since 1954 several fellowships have been of great assistance. In addition to poetry, he has written articles, chiefly for *The Nation,* and radio scripts for the BBC. He has lived in Spain, England, France, Mexico and Hawaii, as well as New York City. His books of poetry are *A Mask for Janus* (1952), *The Dancing Bears* (1954), *Green with Beasts* (1956), *The Drunk in the Furnace* (1960), *The Moving Target* (1963), *The Lice* (1967), *The Carrier of Ladders* (1970) for which he was awarded the Pulitzer Prize, *Writings to an Unfinished Accompaniment* (1973), *The Compass Flower* (1977), *Opening the Hand* (1983), *Selected Poems* (1988) and *The Rain in the Trees* (1988), His translations include *The Poem of the Cid* (1959), *Spanish Ballads* (1960), *The Satires of Persius* (1960), *Lazarillo de Tormes* (1962), *The Song of Roland* (1963), *Selected Translations 1948–1968* (1968), for which he won the P.E.N. Translation Prize for 1968, *Transparence of the World,* a translation of his selection of poems by Jean Follain (1969), *Osip Mandelstam, Selected Poems* (with Clarence Brown) (1974) and *Selected Translations 1968–1978.* He has also published three books of prose, *The Miner's Pale Children* (1970), *Houses and Travellers* (1977) and *Unframed Originals* (1982). In 1974 he was awarded The Fellowship of the Academy of American Poets.

A NOTE ON THE TYPE

This book was set on the Linotype in Janson, a recutting made direct from type cast from matrices long thought to have been made by the Dutchman Anton Janson, who was a practicing type founder in Leipzig during the years 1668–1687. However, it has been conclusively demonstrated that these types are actually the work of Nicholas Kis (1650–1702), a Hungarian, who most probably learned his trade from the master Dutch type founder Dirk Voskens. The type is an excellent example of the influential and sturdy Dutch types that prevailed in England up to the time William Caslon (1692–1766) developed his own incomparable designs from them.

COMPOSITION, PRINTING AND BINDING BY
HERITAGE PRINTERS, INC., CHARLOTTE, NORTH CAROLINA
DESIGNED BY HARRY FORD